3D
Florence

A 72-hour definitive guide on what to see, eat and enjoy in Florence, Italy

3 DAY CITY GUIDES

Copyright © 2015 BeautyBodyStyle, LLC
All rights reserved. No part of this book may be reproduced in any form or by any electronic or mechanical means including information storage and retrieval systems – except in the case of brief quotations in articles or reviews – without the permission in writing from its publisher.

Although the author and publisher have made every effort to ensure that the information in this book was correct at press time, the author and publisher do not assume and hereby disclaim any liability to any party for any loss, damage, or disruption caused by errors or omissions, whether such errors or omissions result from negligence, accident, or any other cause.

Contents

Introduction to Florence	iv
Florence Districts	20
How Not to Get Lost in Florence	24
Florence Day One	28
Florence Day Two	36
Florence Day Three	42
Where to Head Out	46

Cont'd

Local Cuisine in Florence	**50**
Where to Eat	**54**
Where to Stay	**58**
Florence Travel Essentials	**62**
Italian Language Essentials	**66**
Florence Top 20 Things to Do	**74**
Conclusion	**80**

Introduction to Florence

View of Via dei Banchi

Ah, Florence. A city of art. The attic of the Renaissance. A place where romance hangs like a cloud above the Arno River and along the cobbled streets where many of the world's artistic geniuses once strolled.

There are a million reasons to visit Florence, but even if you're only there for the gelato, there is no escaping the art. The layout and architecture of the city is art itself, with the Duomo--the city's main cathedral--- rendering itself king of the skyline above a million terra-cotta roofs.

There's Michelangelo's *David,* Botticelli's *Birth of Venus*, and Leonardo's self-portrait. But there is also art in the sights, scenes and smells of Florence—in the markets, the outdoor cafes, in the way your waiter pours your wine.

Whether you have a week or just a day, no one leaves Florence empty handed. It overflows with passion for all the good things in life. You'll have your fill of pasta and piazzas, art and architecture and you'll leave with memories of the Arno, a new leather jacket and the feeling that you want to come back one day to do it all again.

History

To trace the history of Florence, you must page back to the days of the Romans in 59 BC. There is certainly evidence pointing to earlier occupation by the Etruscans, but what you see today bears the imprint of the Romans in the days of Caesar. Set along the confluence of the Arno and the Mugnone, the city was built rectangular in shape and was enclosed with a wall for protection.

Roman cities were almost always characterized by straight roads which crossed at right angles, with two main roads leading to a central square. In Florence, the main roads lead to the Piazza della Republica where you'll find the Duomo today---still the center of city life.

Thanks to the rich, fertile farmland that surrounds Florence, and its location between Rome and northern Italy, Florence grew steadily from a small Roman settlement into a bustling commercial center. In the 3rd century AD, it was established as the capital of Tuscany, but its success was also often its downfall.

The Byzantines and the German Ostrogoths competed for control of Italy and bustling Florence was seen as a prize. Peace was eventually restored of Italy until 1870 when it was superseded by Rome.

The Florence we see today was built over the old Roman city which makes even its subterranean landscape a treasure trove. It continues to thrive as a banking power, and maintains its reputation as a city of great historical and artistic significance.

Climate and Seasons of Florence

The Tuscany region enjoys a mild climate which makes it a great destination any time of year. In fact, the whole country of Italy makes a lot of best climate lists, thanks to its warm, dry summers and mild winters.

While it's easy to generalize the weather in the Tuscany region, there are some variations based on geography. Along the coast and in the valleys, it tends to be warmer than the hilly regions. That might sound good to people who are visiting from colder regions, but keep in mind summer temperatures can be a bit stifling—not helped at all by the high humidity.

In the winter months, Florence gets cold--- depending on your definition of cold. The city averages 50 degrees in winter, which for many visitors, is pretty comfortable. The coldest month is January.

Undoubtedly, the hottest months are July and August when temperatures can top off in the high 80's or low 90's.

Spring and autumn usually invite more rain.

and the city began to prosper again under the rule of Charlemagne in 774.

It's wasn't until the 11th century that Florence began to sketch its rich historical outline and to succeed as a city both politically and economically. By the 15th century, it reached the pinnacle of its splendor, thanks in part to the presence of its architectural geniuses such as Filippo Brunelleschi and Leon Battista Alberti. Painters such as Masaccio and Botticelli, and the sculptors Donatello and Michelangelo and masters like Leonardo da Vinci also helped to put Florence on the map and they lent their romance to the aura and intrigue of Florence---a romance that persists today.

Florence was notably ground zero for the Renaissance. Although this period in history was pervasive throughout Europe, no one did the Renaissance quite like Florence. Thanks to its thriving economy and the presence of its infamous architects, philosophers, writers and painters, Florence was truly the model of Renaissance culture.

Throughout the 14th to 16th century, the city maintained a strong reputation for artistic innovation. A dozen artists' guilds dotted the city, and Florence exported huge amounts of high quality wool and other textiles throughout Europe.

Around the 15th century, the powerful Medici family abolished the republican government and took over rule. They remained in power until the dynasty died out in 1737. Power was then passed to the Lorraine family, and they ruled until 1861 when Florence was annexed to the Kingdom of Italy during unification. Florence remained the political and cultural capital

Temperatures cool in the autumn, and many people say that October is the perfect time to visit.

Thanks to its river valley location, spring comes early to Florence. Humidity traps warm weather in the city, so by early March it's often warm enough to sunbathe. Early April often boasts clear skies, and mid-70-degree days and the humidity is blessedly low.

Take a look at the average temperatures for Florence by the month:

Average Temperature by Month

January High 50 °F (10 °C), Low 34 °F (1 °C)

February High 53 °F (12 °C), Low 37 °F (3 °C)

March High 59 °F (15 °C), Low 40 °F (4 °C)

April High 65 °F (18 °C), Low 45 °F (7 °C)

May High 74 °F (23 °C), Low 52 °F (11 °C)

June High 81 °F (27 °C), Low 58 °F (14 °C)

July High 88 °F (31 °C), Low 63 °F (17 °C)

August High 87 °F (31 °C), Low 62 °F (17 °C)

September High 79 °F (26 °C), Low 57 °F (14 °C)

October High 70 °F (21 °C), Low 50 °F (10 °C)

November High 58 °F (14 °C), Low 41 °F (5 °C)

December High 50 °F (10 °C), Low 36 °F (2 °C)

Best Time to Visit to Florence

The best time to visit Firenze (the Italian name for Florence) will depend upon your preferences. Are you looking for the best weather or the best deals? Are you hoping to include popular festivals or would you prefer to scour the galleries when the crowds are less dense?

Generally, the most popular time to visit Florence is during the summer. Here's the takeaway on summer: Florence is hot this time of year, and its prime tourist season. On the flipside, it's also the driest season, and a good time for vacationing families. Hotels and attractions tend to be more expensive during this busy season, but travelers enjoy the endless outdoor cafes and the ambience of summer which includes Florence's famous outdoor festivals.

Of all the summer months, August is the least crowded. However, some restaurants and shops close during this month for summer vacation.

There are those who prefer to visit Italy in the winter months when the crowds are at their thinnest. It may be the coldest time of year, but it is also the least expensive time to travel. Beyond the monetary savings and the presence of fewer tourists, there are other good reasons to visit Florence in the winter. The air is brisk and the light is said to be lovely, making it a favorite time for photographers to visit. In the evenings, the city shines with an endless stream of lights strung across the streets in a gleaming, festive canopy. And the traditional rustic dishes served in Florence will warm your soul. You can sit in a warm café and feast on hearty soups and thick pasta sauces—a nice retreat in chilly weather.

Spring also represents an alternative to the popular summer season. By mid-April, the cafes are opening up their patios and outdoor bars. Since spring comes early to the city, the weather is warm and the days are growing longer. May is also a favorite for many repeat travelers to Firenze who like to get there before the hot summer temperatures arrive, but keep in mind the spring also experiences rain.

October and early November are also great months for travel through Tuscany. The temperatures are mild, the sun hasn't made an exit just yet and the humidity lessens.

Here's a breakdown of the seasons and their festivals:

April

It's spring! Temperatures range from 45 to 65 degree Fahrenheit, so layering is necessary. In April, the sun is bright but you still have a good chance of scoring a good deal on flights and hotels. Pack a good rain jacket as there is a good chance you may experience some rain.

Festivals:

Maggio Musicale Fiorentino (April-June)

May-September

In the summer months, Florence comes alive. Tourists spend hours at open-air restaurants and outdoor bars. Expect temperatures to be in the upper 80's and be sure to book your room early as this is a busy time of year for tourism.

Festivals:

Maggio Musicale Fiorentino (April-June)

Fochi di San Giovanni (June)

Calcio in Costume (June)

November-March

The winter months see cold temperatures and fewer tourists. Expect the days to be between and 30 and 50 degrees. There are fewer lines at major attractions and hotel rates are reduced.

Festivals:

Florence Biennale (December)

Fashion Shows (January)

October

Considered a lovely time to visit Florence. Mild weather with warm days and barely chilly nights. Temperatures average in the low 70's. The summer tourist season is over.

Language

It's a good idea to get to know the language of any country you intend to visit—even if it's just a few words or phrases. The good news is that Italian is a beautiful, poetic language and it's not too hard to learn some simple words. It evolved from the vernacular of ancient Rome and has a fascinating transformative history.

Europe was once a pandemonium of endless dialects derived from Latin, and Italy was no exception, since it was made up of different city states. It was hard for a merchant in Florence to communicate with a business owner from Rome.

But when Italian unification became a reality in 1861, it was clear that the country needed one decisive language. Italian intellectuals gathered and chose Florence's dialect as Italy's official language. And which Florentine dialect did they settle on? The one spoken by the great poet Dante Alighieri.

And while Italian is spoken by just 62 million people worldwide, it is the fourth most popular language in the world.

It's also a good idea to buy a small language book you can carry around with you that translates Italian words to English and vice versa (common travel phrases are included in this guide, or download one to your smart phone or electronic tablet. It's also important to note that as the English language becomes almost mandatory in the global business world, it becomes easier to travel the world and get along with simple English and some basic gesturing---especially in the markets where most merchants know some rudimentary English.

Getting to Florence

It's not a big secret that traveling to Italy from the United States and other non-European countries doesn't come cheap. In fact, nothing in Italy is cheap, from hotels to souvenirs and meals.

For most people, airfare will top the list as one of the greatest expenses for their Italian vacation. If money is an issue, there are a few tips that can help you save on your flights:

> Avoid the busiest tourist months which run between the end of spring and the beginning of fall.
>
> Put some time and energy into researching your flights. One day airfare will cost a king's ransom, and the next day you'll spy a greatly reduced fare. The best day to look for flights in the US is on a Tuesday at 3:00 pm. That's when a lot of airlines post their bargains.
>
> If at all possible, have flexible dates. Weekend travel is more expensive than midweek travel. If you can maintain some flexibility within the span of a few days, you might find better deals.
>
> Price a flight to a capital outside of Italy and then take one of Europe's bargain airlines (like Ryanair) into Italy. You may be able to score some big savings this way, although it doesn't

score high on the convenience factor.

When it comes to getting to Florence, many people fly into Rome and take the train to Florence. Sometimes this can represent significant savings, and trains in Europe are an extremely dependable method of transportation. Be sure to figure out whether taking a train to Florence is actually cheaper, as occasionally you'll find flying to be the better deal, especially if you're booked straight through.

Florence is 173 miles north of Rome, and since these are two of the most popular cities in the country, there are frequent trains that run directly between them from the Rome Termini Station and the Florence Santa Maria Novella Station. Some regional trains also leave from Roma Tiburtina.

Frecce trains are direct and provide the fastest (and most expensive) transportation to Florence from Rome---about one hour and thirty minutes. You'll need to reserve a seat on these trains ahead of time. Less expensive trains (regional trains that make a series of stops) take two to four hours. In general, trains leave from early morning until about 10:30 pm.

You can check current Rome-to-Florence schedules and ticket prices on the Trenitalia web site (www.trenitalia.com or www.raileurope.com). People in the US may find it easier and more convenient to buy tickets ahead of time through Select Italy, a travel site that provides information on just about anything you might need to plan your trip, from train tickets, to museum tickets to side trips.

Visit www.SelectItaly.com.

Also note there is a private, high-speed train that leaves from Rome's Ostiense and Tiburtina stations (not Termini) that has a direct route to Florence. You can buy **Italo** train tickets in US dollars online through Select Italy.

If you decide to take the train to Florence from Rome, you'll need to get from the airport to one of Rome's train stations (the most common being the Termini station). You can take a cab, hire a private car beforehand or take the bus or train.

The Leonardo Express is the direct train that serves the route between the airport and the center of the city of Rome and it leaves every 30 minutes. Be sure to study the route so you know when you need to exit the train at the Termini station.

Buses

This will be your cheapest option for getting from the airport to the train station in Rome. The Roma Airport Bus costs about 4 euros and makes 23 trips daily between the airport and the city center. Visit www.romeairportbus.com for more information.

Another convenient bus service is called T.A.M. and costs about 5 euros per person. It runs between the airport and the Termini train station where most trains depart to Florence. Hours of operation are between 08:00 am and 11:30 pm. They also stop near Ostiense train station for those who are connecting to Florence and points north via the Italo high-speed train. The buses depart from Terminal 3 at the airport.

The Terravision Shuttle and the SIT Airport Bus are also options for getting to the Termini station or into Rome's center. If you have the time, these less costly options are often a convenient—if not more adventurous—way to get to Florence from Rome.

Taxi

You'll pay for the convenience of a taxi (with a fixed rate of 48 euros) to the Termini station. Taxis hold up to four people and their luggage. If you're staying in Rome for a few days and your hotel is outside of this general area, you'll have to pay what's on the meter. You can check out http://www.comune.roma.it/PCR/resources/cms/documents/tariffario_taxi_luglio_2012.pdf for more information.

Note that the fixed price from the airport to central Rome applies only to taxis licensed by the City of Rome. You'll find the taxis have the city council's crest (SPQR) painted on the doors. Other taxis, such as those licensed by the Comune of Fiumicino, can charge by their meter. Insist on taking a Roman taxi: they now have the fixed rate to and from the airport printed on their doors and you always know what you're getting and exactly how much it costs.

If you are travelling as a group of four, a taxi is cheaper than the Leonardo Express train and you'll avoid having to lug your suitcases to the train.

Private Car

A private car and driver will cost 50 euros for up to three people. For about the same money as a taxi, you can have a driver waiting at the exit near customs at FCO or at your door in Rome. It's best to do your own research, but check out www.romecabs.com and www.romeshuttlelimousine.com as a starting point.

Keep in mind that private car services usually charge more if there are more than two or three people in the group. Also, avoid any car or shuttle service that requires payment in advance. In most cases, the reliable companies ask for payment after they have provided the service.

A note about tipping: Tipping is not required in Italy, but it is certainly fine to give a small tip for good service. 10 percent is a good amount if you've received excellent service.

Airlines that Fly to Florence from Rome

People with limited time may want to continue on to Florence directly from their flight into Rome or another Italian city. Here is a list of some of the airlines that fly from Rome to Florence if you're not booked straight through from your home city:

Air Berlin

Alitalia

Austrian Airlines

Brussels Airlines

Darwin Airline

KLM

Lufthansa

Luxair

Swiss

Vueling Airlines

Rent a Car

It's nice to know that in an age of "so much to do, so little time," some people still opt for the slow boat. Renting a car to get to Florence is a wonderful way to see some of the Tuscan countryside and to appreciate the journey there rather than just zipping through it. The trip takes about three hours without stops, but there are some great villages and sites to see along the way if you have the time.

It's easy to book a car through one of your favorite travel sites on the internet, and maps can be purchased ahead of time through agencies like AAA or Michelin.

Plan to make a few stops along the way. The beautiful and ancient Etruscan city of Orvieto lies right on the main route between Rome and Florence and boasts some compelling Etruscan archaeological sites. It's the perfect place to stop for lunch.

And don't miss Sienna---a town rich with Renaissance art and architecture. Its unfinished cathedral is a site to behold and you'll find some wonderful spots for a latte or lunch.

Tips for renting a car in Italy include:

Book early from home.

Research! Compare fares at internet travel sites and then see if you can get a better price at autoeurope.com. They are similar to a consolidator and frequently have low prices.

Make sure you understand the total daily rate, since car rentals like to stick it to you with an array of extra fees. Also note that Italy has a mandatory collision waiver and theft protection fee which will add to your daily rate.

Don't rent more than you need. Bigger cars are hard to park and maneuver near city centers.

You probably don't need a car for your entire trip. If you're staying in Rome the first four days of your trip, forget about a car rental until you're ready to leave. You don't need to drive to the important sites in Rome. And this goes for all major cities including Florence, Palermo, Milan, etc.

Consider a rail-and-drive pass. It's a great budget tool that mixes your choice of three to five train days plus two days of a Hertz rental car (with additional car days available for $66–$226 each, depending on size and type of car). It's great for a trip where you're mixing it up. For example: Say you fly into Rome, take a train to Naples, then pick up a rental car to head to the Tuscan hills. Later, you take a train to Venice but drive to Milan to catch your flight home. Check out www.raileurope.com for more information on rail-and-drive passes.

Getting Around Florence

The key to getting around Florence is to have a good pair of walking shoes. Cars are not allowed in the pedestrian zone where most of the hotels are located, so it doesn't really pay to have a rental car unless you're crazy. If you do have a car because you're traveling through Italy and stopping in Florence, you may want to book a hotel outside of the pedestrian zone where your car will be welcome. (If you're just coming in for the day, we list some options below.)

Your other option is to find a paid parking lot or a private garage. Tips for finding parking options can be found at www.visitflorence.com. (They even have some tips on finding free parking.) Your hotel is also a valuable resource, as they may have a special deal with a particular parking garage for their guests. Daily rates are generally 20 euros or more.

The historic center of Florence is a Limited Traffic Zone (ZTL). The fines for driving in this zone are very high if you enter without having the necessary permit. The hours of the ZTL are between 7:30am and 7:30pm on weekdays and 7:30am to 6pm on Saturdays.

You are, however, allowed to unload your baggage at your hotel, but then you must immediately exit the ZTL and park outside of its parameters. Your hotel will let the police know your license plate number so it can be taken off the list of cars to be fined as you unload. If it all sounds a bit daunting, it is meant to. But you'll appreciate these restrictions when you're walking around a historic center that is free of cars.

The historic center of Florence is relatively small,

so walking is the way to go. There is also a fleet of electronic busses in Florence that can help you get to key tourist areas. You probably won't need the bus, but instructions are provided below.

Maps are readily available at the five tourist centers in the historic district, so be sure to pick one up to help plan your days. The map will also help you to identify where you can find the city busses.

Taxis

Taxis are also easy to find in Florence. Keep in mind, you can't flag a taxi as you do in many places in the United States and elsewhere. Taxis are stationed at special parking stands in most of the major squares in Italian cities and in Florence, and they can also be requested by phone. Ask your hotel concierge or restaurant host to call a taxi for you.

Fares and rates are listed inside the cab so be sure to check them to make sure the fare you are charged is correct. Most fares within the city center range from 3 to 6 euros.

The fare from the airport in Florence to the city center is fixed at 20 euros.

To check out a fee table (as taxi prices are set by city officials) visit http://www.comune.fi.it/opencms/export/sites/retecivica/materiali/hp_amministrazione/TariffarioTaxi.pdf.

Buses

City buses in Florence are orange or deep purple

and white. Tickets can be purchased from authorized sales dealers anywhere where an ATAF sticker is found—usually on a window in coffee shops, newsstands, etc.

The busses have three doors: The front and back are for getting on and the middle door is used to exit the bus. When you get on, make sure to validate your ticket in the ticket validation machine on the bus which will print the date and time on the ticket. Your ticket is only good for 90 minutes. The same ticket can be used on multiple busses within that time period. The fine for not having a valid tickets cost 45 euros, and it's been said they don't have much sympathy for naïve visitors. Tickets can also be purchased directly from the driver, though it will cost you a little more. A 90-minute bus ticket costs 1.20 euros.

Florence Districts

1

Piazza del Pesce Street sign

The lovely Florence is the capital city of Italy's Tuscany region. It is the most populous city in this region and stretches 40 square miles in size, making it pretty small for such a lively city. One can easily walk from one end to the other in less than just 30 minutes. Florence is divided into five major districts namely, The **Piazza Della Duomo**, **Piazza Della Signoria**, **Oltrarno**, **Castello** and **Piazza Della Reppublica**.

Piazza Della Duomo

This square marks Florence's religious heart as a home to the Cathedral of Santa Maria del Fiore, **Brunelleschi's Dome, Giotto's Bell Tower, the Baptistery of San Giovanni, the Crypt of Santa Reparata and the Opera Museum.** It goes without saying that you have not seen Florence if you haven't seen these majestic historical monuments.

Piazza Della Signoria

The main train station is situated in Piazza Della Signoria and right across from it is the famous Santa Maria Novella church which contains great artwork, sharing the same name as the station. Surrounded by the most important buildings in Florence, this square is a place of incomparable beauty and elegance. Visitors can look forward to a collection of contemporary Italian Art from well-known painters and sculptors.

The Oltrarno

A walk through the Oltrarno takes in three very different aspects of Florence that cannot be missed: The splendor and riches of the mammoth Palazzo Pitti, the gracious Giardino di Boboli; and the charm of the Oltrarno itself. This is a proud working-class neighborhood with artisans and antiques shops. If jewelry shopping is on your list, then you are in for a treat in the Oltrarno.

Castello

This neighborhood is situated in the hills of Florence, not too far from the City's airport. It boasts with an elegant villa known as the Medici Villa and its splendid Italian garden. The garden's many statues and fountains make it popular to tourists, the Cave of animals and other smaller secret gardens make this an enjoyable quiet time during your visit in Florence.

Piazza Della Repubblica

No visit to Florence is quite complete without passing by this intriguing architectural square that is alive and buzzing with cafes and street artists. While in Piazza Della Repubblica one can leisurely take in Florentine life on the Ponte Vecchio, also known as the Old Bridge; the view of Florence from the highest point of the bridge is breathtaking. There's also trade and artisan shops along this lovely bridge walkway.

Recommended Walking Tours

Artisans and Shopping

This tour is a walk-through the City's workshops. Get an in depth understanding of the creativity behind Florence's traditionally handcrafted products.

http://www.walksinsideflorence.it/artisans-and-shopping.html

The Medici Family Tour

This is a 3 hour tour within the Palace's exterior and interior. It focuses on the Medici family and the vast relationship between political power and art.

http://www.walksinsideflorence.it/the-medici-family-tour-their-palace-and-district.html

2
How Not to Get Lost in Florence

Santa Maria Novella train station

One can easily get carried away in such a beautiful city and wander off from the crowds. If this happens, there's no need to panic as the city of Florence is quite closely knit together.

Most tourist attractions are centrally located and literally walking distance apart. With so many majestic buildings to use as landmarks it isn't much of a hassle to pinpoint your location and navigate. The most famous landmarks in Florence are the Cathedral, Uffizi Gallery, Palazzo Vecchio, the Ponte Vecchio Bridge and Piazza della Signoria.

One could use the tall buildings as central meeting places such as the Duomo or the Bell Tower. They dominate the city's skyline and are therefore very easy to locate. Many hotels in the city also offer publications and maps to assist in finding your way. There are also information offices within the city to help you stay on track. Key locations include within the train station, opposite the train station in Piazza della Stazione and near the Duomo on Via Cavour.

Moving around Florence by taxi is different from other cities, you cannot hail on the streets for one; you can either call one directly or go to a specifically marked taxi stop. Safe parking zones for those who prefer to drive may be found in the city's maps, it is also useful to understand obvious road signs like North or South, Slow Down, Exit etc. Buses move around at specific times from different points of the city, they can be found at the Santa Maria Novella train station, opposite the church. If you are not sure where to get off just ask the driver.

Although getting lost in Florence is highly unlikely, plan in advance and always carry a map in hand, just in case you lose your way.

Doors Gates of Paradise by Lorenzo Ghiberti, Baptistery of St. John.

3

Florence
Day One

Florence Duomo (Santa Maria del Fiore)

If there's one thing that's true about Florence it's that you can spend an entire month there and not see it all. But you can certainly pack its greatest treasures into a couple of days.

This itinerary is ideal for the first-time traveler who wants to be sure they see and do as much as they possibly can in the span of three days. Of course, depending on the number of days you have and what your interests are, you can rearrange the itinerary as much as you like, but see this as an important overview of the best that Florence has to offer, as well as some jewels that are off the beaten track.

Before leaving home, be sure to book your tickets to the Uffuzi Museum and the Academia because you don't want to lose precious time waiting in line. Tickets can be purchased directly from the gallery online (www.uffizi.org and www.accademia.org) or at other sites on the internet like SelectItaly.

com. You'll pay a bit more when you purchase your tickets ahead of time, but it is well worth it.

Day 1

Today is the day to get some of the big things out of the way, and to stand and marvel at some of the smaller things---like renowned Renaissance art. Today is all about introducing yourself to Florence: sipping latte, walking through piazzas, and getting a grand view of the city from above.

The first thing you want to do (whether starting fresh in the morning or as soon as you check into your hotel) is visit the Duomo—the beautiful cathedral that dominates the skyline in Florence. Climb to the top of the dome for an unparalleled view of the city. The beautiful baptistery adjacent to the dome has beautiful tile mosaics and impressive, massive bronze doors which have earned their name as the *Gates of Paradise*. You may want to take a guided tour of the entire site. Ticket booths for entry and tours are clearly marked.

If it's early and you haven't eaten breakfast at your hotel, you may want to stop for a bite to eat before or after exploring the Duomo. Keep in mind, Italians don't sit down to eat breakfast. They have breakfast standing up at latte bars where they enjoy a quick biscotti. All you really have to do in the mornings to eat like an Italian is to follow your nose to the nearest bakery or café which open early in the morning.

If you're intent on having an American breakfast, there are several places that will cater to your bacon and egg fix. To eat breakfast like an Italian, check out **Sergiobar**, which is located in the Piazza Del Duomo. (Address: Piazza del Duomo 59r) If you insist on a full American breakfast, then **The Diner** may be your place for the next three days. They serve up bacon, eggs and pancakes to American tourists who miss their morning staples. (Address: Via dell'Acqua, 2)

After leaving the Duomo, head over to the animated **Piazza della Signoria**, which has served as the cultural, political and social heart of Florence since the 13th century. This is where Florentines go to hang out with friends and chat. You can spend more than an hour marveling at the sites inside the square, or simply just people watch.

Within the square, check out the **Loggia de' Lanzi**—the magnificent outdoor sculpture gallery where some notable and original works of art are displayed from the Renaissance era.

The Kidnapping of the Sabine Women by Giambologna

Then walk over to the Old Palace on the left—**The Palazzo Vecchio**---a late 13th century fortress which still serves as city hall.

Ornate courtyard in the Palazzo Vecchio

In front of the city hall, you'll spy a raised platform called the ***aringaria.*** Orators once addressed crowds here during times of political crisis, which by all accounts was quite often. Be sure to check out the life-size copy of Michelangelo's *David* in this area and Baccio Bandinelli's *Heracles*. Just off to the north in the corner of Palazzo Vecchio is the massive Neptune Fountain, carved by Ammanati in 1576.

Before heading into the **Uffizi Gallery**, you may want to stop for a latte, lunch or a snack. There is no shortage of restaurants and cafes near the piazza, but Vini e Vecchi Sapori is a hidden gem open for lunch and dinner.

View of Uffizi Gallery from Piazza della Signoria

(Address: Via Dei Magazzini 3R) Their homemade dishes get rave reviews—and it's even recommended by one of Florence's illustrious cooking schools. (If you don't manage lunch here today, you may want to stop in and book dinner reservations for later in your trip.)

Spent the rest of the afternoon in the Uffizi Gallery right here in the piazza. This is a must-see on your list, and since you booked your tickets ahead of time (www.Uffizi.org) there will be no time wasted waiting in line.

The Uffizi Gallery is, of course, one of the oldest and most famous art museums in the world, boasting a renowned collection of paintings and sculptures from a span of centuries. It includes works by Botticelli, da Vinci, Michelangelo and Raphael.

There are some different options for tackling this important gallery: You can sign up for a guided tour with an art history expert who can help put what you're seeing into context, or navigate the gallery on your own. If you chose the latter, it's a good idea to become familiar with the gallery by visiting the Uffizi website for a breakdown of the artwork and exhibits before you leave home so your time is well spent.

Keep in mind the gallery closes at 6:50 pm and is closed on Mondays—as are most museums in Florence. There are three types of admission tickets, but most people will fall under general admission guidelines unless you are a student, handicapped or under the age of 25.

If you're ready for dinner after visiting the gallery, you won't be sorry if you head to **Coquinarius**—a place even the locals love. (Address: Via dell'Oche, 11/R) Their food is fabulous. (Try their rustic salad and the pear ravioli.) They're known for their fresh and innovative dishes and you'll find a great selection of wine there.

Tired yet? Grab a gelato on your way back to the hotel. Gelato is an art form in Italy. With too many to list, a few gelaterios that make the top ten are **Grom**, **Gelateria La Carraia** and **Carapina.**

3 Day City Guides

Gelato in Florence, Italy

// 4

Florence
Day Two

Michelangelo's David

Dig a little deeper today into the art and history of Florence by spending time in must-see churches and galleries and by crossing the Arno to watch artisans creating the traditional crafts of Florence. You'll end the day in a beautiful palace followed by a light meal at one of the city's most beloved restaurants.

Grab a quick latte and a biscotti this morning and then head to the **Galleria dell' Accademia** just before it opens to see Michelangelo's *David*. This is sage advice, as the crowds swell early and persist throughout the day. (Be sure to buy your tickets ahead of time at www.accademia.org.)

Michelangelo's most famous work was carved from a single block of marble, and upon its completion in 1504, was symbolized as a powerful icon of Florentine power from its perch in front of the Palazzo Vecchio.

You'll find other works by Michelangelo in the

gallery. Adjoining rooms showcase paintings by Andrea Orcagna, Taddeo Gaddi, Domenico Ghirlandaio, Filippino Lippi and Sandro Botticelli.

Interior of Santa Maria Novella

Before lunch, head to the nearby **Basilica de Santa Maria Novella** to see a stunning frescoed chapel and a host of artistic masterpieces. The true highlights are found behind the main alter--- Domenico Ghirlandaio's frescoes that relate the lives of the Virgin Mary, and frescoes by Niccolò di Tommaso and Nardo di Cione located upstairs.

Now is a great time to head toward the center of town to visit the famous medieval bridge **Ponte Vecchio** to have lunch and shop. Until 1218, this was the only bridge that crossed the Arno River and it has stubbornly survived infamous wars and floods. There have been shops on the bridge since the 13th century and initially they included an array of

Ponte Vecchio over the Arno River

merchants including butchers and fishmongers. But in 1593, Ferdinand I decided only goldsmiths and jewelers could keep shops there and that's what you'll find there today. By walking across, though, you'll find the artisan quarter (called Oltrarno) where old traditions and fine craftsmanship are on display.

You'll find some wonderful restaurants in the area, but Il Latini is truly a standout. (Address: Via dei Palchetti 6R) It's the real deal when it comes to eating in Florence and your waiter will be happy to order for you so you don't miss their specialties.

The Florentine steak?

Indescribable.

After lunch, spend the rest of the afternoon over the bridge in Oltrarno looking for specialty marbled paper and other traditional crafts. You'll find the Medici's grand **Pitti Palace** in this neighborhood with its fabulous painting galleries and beautiful gardens.

View of Uffizi Gallery from Piazza della Signoria

If you're in the mood for a light dinner this evening, check out Cantinetta dei Verrazzano (address: Via dei Tavolini 18-20r) which is a much beloved spot that offers lighter fare.

3 Day City Guides

View of Florence from Boboli Gardens (Giardino di Boboli)

5

Florence Day Three

Colorful ceilingin Basilica di Santa Croce

Tie up loose ends today by visiting the rest of the must-see spots of Florence. After a hearty breakfast, you'll pay homage to Michelangelo and other greats in their final resting place, and then head up the hill to get a beautiful view of the city from an original medieval church. After lunch, it's time to do your own thing---whether it's shopping for leather jackets or taking a cooking class or seeing one last church.

Have a hearty breakfast this morning at Astor Café near the Duomo. (Address: Piazza Duomo 20/r) and then head to **Santa Croce Church** which is the final resting place of Michelangelo, Galileo, Rossini and Machiavelli. (You couldn't be in better company.)

Then head skyward to **Piazzale Michelangelo** for another unparalleled view off the city. There, you'll find Florence's only Romanesque church perched on a hill above the city. The church is quite unique and its interior stands as a true example of medieval

View of the Florence from Piazzale Michelangelo

architecture---basically unaltered since 1163.

This afternoon is a good time to indulge your interests. If you plan ahead, an afternoon cooking class would be an excellent way to end your trip. Try **Giovanni's Italian Cooking Class** (www.Florencecookingclass.com), or do some of your own research online to find a class that sparks your interest.

As you're strolling the streets, you'll also often find signs on storefronts and buildings pointing to cooking classes inside. Booking at least a day ahead is a good idea.

If shopping is on your agenda, try the **leather district** which is the place to haggle for knock-off Gucci scarves, marbleized paper products, souvenirs, and of course—leather. Leather jackets and belts and boots are often the gifts tourists like to leave with and the leather district is a good place to get a deal. (This is a good time to remind you to watch for pickpockets. Petty theft is a reality in Florence—and indeed all over Italy—so keep your cash and documents in a money belt under your shirt and *not* in a back pocket or purse.)

And here is an absolute must: Visit the **San Lorenzo Central Market** near the leather market and shop for food like a real Italian. The market is one of the oldest in Florence and there's two floors of fruits, vegetables, artisan cheeses, prosciutto, olives and all the things that make Italy a culinary tour de force.

Art lovers may want to return to the Uffizi Gallery or wander along the medieval streets to look for works by local artists.

If you haven't had your fill of churches, two more make the must-see lists: **The Church of Santo Spirito** (in the plaza by the same name) with its many treasures and the **San Lorenzo Church** and chapels where the Medici family worshipped and found their final resting place. (Located in the Piazza San Lorenzo.)

And there's certainly nothing wrong with just parking yourself at an outdoor café and watching the world go by for an afternoon. Sometimes it's a good thing to just simply *be* in Florence and not just *do.*

6

Where to Head Out

View of Ponte Vecchio at night

Looking for a pleasant place to have a cocktail or hear a little music at night? (Young club-goers should skip this section and move on to the next). Here are some hip spots to spend a little time long after the sun goes down:

The **Cocktail Bar** is near the Duomo and pours a great Moscow Mule. Great ambiance here. (Vai delle Oche 15R)

Don't miss **Harry's Bar** located next to the river. (Lungarno Vespucci, 22r) Mature patrons, great drinks.

Rooftop cocktails in a swanky atmosphere. And even better, it's next to the Ponte Vecchio. Great view, great drinks. On the roof of the **Hotel Continental. (**Vicolo dell'Oro, 6R)

If you're into the **party scene** Florence doesn't disappoint. There's certainly more to Firenze than Renaissance art.

Here are some of the best-known **clubs** in town for the younger set:

Club TwentyOne: It's all about the dance floor here. Cheap drinks, unpretentious décor and late nights. (Via Cimatori 13)

Yab: This is the place to wear your new designer threads. It's glam. It's hip. And it has a great dance floor. (Via dè Sassetti, 5/R)

Space Electronic: Guess what? They have electronic music here. The downstairs is for flirting; the upstairs is for dancing. (Via Palazzuolo, 37)

Twice: Trendy, yes. Upscale, yes. But people say the atmosphere is laid back and friendly. (Via Giuseppe Verdi, 57r)

Blob: Nights here start early and go late. It's got an art-house vibe and a cozy dance floor. (Via Vinegia, 21)

3 Day City Guides

Aperol spritz

7

Local Cuisine in Florence

Traditional antipasti

Like most Italian cuisine, Florentine dishes are deliciously simple and locally produced; with the most common pairing being that of mellow cheeses and flavorful grilled meats. Be sure to add white beans cooked with sage and olive oil to your culinary itinerary, along with thick and hearty soups that feature tender bites of meat; namely boar, deer and rabbit.

Starters in Florence are typically a small portion of either cold meats, fresh vegetables with olive oil, chicken liver crostini, tuna and bean salad or toasted bread with olive oil. Meat appetizers are often accompanied by cheeses, bread or a mixed salad depending on the venue. These starters are excellent appetizers that can be enjoyed best with a glass of wine —ask your waiter for recommendations. Most establishments proudly carry local wines that are both delicious and affordable.

When it comes to main course dishes, pork is a popular ingredient; both fresh and cured are frequented within Florentine cuisine. Sausages are no exception and they are traditionally cooked in their own fat until they turn a warm crispy brown. These sausages can be best enjoyed at any pizzicagnoli shop in Florence, together with dried fish and a variety of cheeses.

Traditional tripe, known in Florence as Trippaio, is also amongst the top local dishes for many visitors. There's also the famous Florentine steak for meat lovers as well as thick and slow-cooked game ragù stews to be enjoyed. Looking for lighter vegetarian fare? Try the pappa con pomodoro, which is a tomato and bread soup, ribollita soup (made from cannellini beans, bread and vegetables) and barley salad.

Wine is openly enjoyed on most corners of the City's streets; one can easily find a "vinaino" (small stand) where you can sip a glass of wine for taste. Overwhelming local desserts include anything from chestnut cakes, sweet grape bread to carnival time biscuits commonly known as Cenci. These tasty little sweets are traditionally served in most restaurants throughout Florence.

Having said the above, food in Florence is simple, hearty and locally produced, it can be enjoyed at extremely reasonable prices. No Florentine cookery is ever without these four fundamental ingredients:

- Bread that is plain, unsalted and well baked
- Extra-virgin olive oil
- Grilled meat or steaks

Wine

Recommended Food Tours/Cooking Classes

Taste Florence, where eating is an art:

Treat your taste buds to all the flavors that Florence has to offer by taking this amazing walk tour. Visit artisan bakers, fall in love with the chocolate makers and cool off with amazing wines.

http://tasteflorence.com/

Wine Tasting in Florence:

Get a taste of local quality wines while enjoying a combination of Italian foods of your choice. You can expect to see bread, local cheeses and liver mousses on the menu.

http://www.aboutflorence.com/wine-in-florence-tuscany.html

Cooking Classes at the Florence Chefs & OLIO – Florence School of Olive Oil:

Practice preparing local dishes with experienced Florentine chefs' in a school that offers great cooking classes. Discover the true secrets behind Italian/Tuscan cooking.

http://www.walksinsideflorence.it/food-market-visit-with-a-cooking-class.html

8

Where to Eat

Pasta alla carbonara with truffles

It would be nice to say that all restaurants are created equal in Florence (it is Florence, after all), but that's not the case. It's just as easy to find yourself in an overpriced restaurant with mediocre food as it is in any city in the world. It pays to do your research. And since eating is such a vital part of any visit to Italy, spend some time comparing restaurants and reading reviews.

Beyond the restaurants mentioned in your three-day itinerary above, there are a plethora of excellent restaurants to choose from. Yet to be mentioned, too, is street food---or small take-out places where you can grab a panini and find a nice spot to eat on a bench somewhere. Picnics are great, too and the Central Market is the place to grab some basic staples—like cheese, bread and fruit. Also worth mentioning are the fabulous wine stores in Florence---whether you're looking for a bottle to take back to your room or you're bringing a few home as gifts.

Restaurants $$$

Some of the best restaurants in Florence are located around Santa Croce and the Oltrarno, but keep in mind that the best Tuscan fare is made with fresh and local ingredients sourced from the surrounding region. Many restaurants are small in Florence so reservations are a must. Your hotel concierge can help.

Enoteca Pinchiorri- If you're looking to splurge one night, this is definitely the treat of a lifetime. Despite its world-wide reputation for Italian-French fusion dishes, it is fancy but not overly pretentious. The atmosphere is charming and full of character and the food is show stopping. (Address: Via Ghibellina, 87)

Ristorante Cibrèo- Creative dishes, unpretentious, and with an ever-changing menu. This restaurant makes many fine dining lists. It's an original—with a varied and interesting menu. (Address: Via de Verrocchio 8r)

Restaurants $$

Ristorante La Giostra- Cozy and authentic ambience. Well-regarded, much loved. Started by a Hapsburg prince and now run by his twin sons. A highlight for many travelers and credited with making many evenings special. The antipasto platter brought to every table is the perfect touch. (Address: 12 Borgo Pinti)

Ristorante Buca Dell'Orafo- Set in the cantina of a palace from the 1200s near the Ponte Vecchio, the food is old style and the menu is full of Tuscan specialties. A favorite of the locals, too. (Address: Via dei Girolami, 28)

Restaurants $

Casa del Vino- A Florence favorite. It's not always easy to get a seat, and there's a reason for that. Sandwiches, paninos, bruschetta---there's something for everyone here and it's all good. Some excellent vintage wines. (Address: 16 via dell'Ariento)

Il Giova - This is a Mom and Pop restaurant where Pop is the loyal chef and Mom serves and collects the money. It's tiny, so you need reservations. The food is great and the chocolate cake is even better. (Address: Via Borgo La Croce, 73)

9
Where to Stay

Spiral staircase in an old house. Florence Italy

You can stay along the banks of the Arno River, or in an elegant room in a grand old palace, in the historic center or outside of it. And thanks to all of the famous landmarks, it's not too hard to find a room with a view.

Hotels *****

Hotel Il Salviatino-A restored 15th century villa on the hillside of Fiesole that offers a stunning view of the city. The only thing that might possibly rival the grandeur of the setting is the impeccable service and the devotion of the staff to help you enjoy the experience of being there. (www.salviatino.com)

Relais Santa Croce-How do you take the elegant past and make it relevant in today's hotel industry? The Relais has done a splendid job showing us how it's done. It offers the modern comforts of luxury in a grand old building right in the historic district. The ambience is amazing, so it's tempting not to leave your room... but you must. (www.relaischateaux.com/santacroce)

Hotels ****

The San Gallo Palace hotel-This new hotel provides an elegant atmosphere with good attention to detail, a beautiful garden and an American bar. Located right in the center of things in the historic district. (Sangallopalace.com)

Brunelleschi Hotel-Very close to the Duomo and housed in a reconstructed 6th-century Byzantine tower and medieval church dating from 1400. If that's not perfect enough, this hotel offers a long list of amenities, like a basement museum, Tiffany-style stained glass window, a roof terrace with a view of the Duomo, complimentary breakfast and a cocktail lounge. It's darn near perfect.

Hotels ***

Hotel Duomo Firenze-You can't beat the location, and this old-style hotel has some great amenities to go along with the view. The rooms are spacious enough, the staff is friendly and the breakfasts are great. (www.hotelduomofirenze.it/)

Hotel Restaurant La Scaletta-Near the Ponte Vecchio, this well-situated hotel is modern, clean and offers breakfast and a lovely rooftop bar. It's a gem in this price range.

Budget **

Hotel David-Great spot for the budget-conscious traveler. Very clean, nicely decorated, this wonderful small hotel offers a free happy hour and mini bar, wonderful staff and great beds. (hoteldavid.com)

Hotel Il Bargellino-Nicely decorated rooms with high ceilings, a common terrace, and a great location near the train station and the historic district. Family run and with a helpful, attentive staff. (www.ilbargellino.com)

10
Florence Travel Essentials

Bicycle along empty street

To eliminate the frustration of travelling to a foreign city, it is important to know a few things pertaining to that country, such as the currency they use, phone calls, meal times etc. Here is a list of essentials that may come in handy while visiting Florence:

Currency

The Euro is the official currency of Italy and therefore used as the main currency in Florence. Hard cash is obtainable at exchange outlets throughout the city; otherwise you can use Visa, MasterCard, Discover or American Express card. While credit card purchases are mainstream, it is advisable to have cash on hand to pay for minor things such as cabs, tips, street vending and those prized market purchases.

Phone Calls

Calling Florence landline from the United States/

Canada:

Dial **011** (exit code) followed by **39** (country code for Italy) then **055** (Florence area code) before finally dialing the **local number**.

011 + 39 + 055 + local number

Calling Florence mobile from the United States/Canada:

Dial **011** (exit code) followed by **39** (country code for Italy) then the **mobile number**.

011 + 39 + local number

Calling Florence landline from Europe/Globally:

Dial **00** followed by **39** (country code for Italy) then **055** (Florence area code) before finally dialing the **local number**.

00 + 39 + 055 + local number

Calling Florence mobile from Europe/Globally:

Dial **00** followed by **39** (country code for Italy) then the **mobile number**.

00 + 39 + local number

When calling from Florence to another country you will simply dial the Italian international prefix (00) followed by the code of the country you are calling.

00 + country code + area code + local number

Local calls within Florence

Landline: **Dial 055 + local number**

Mobile: **Dial 39 + mobile number**

Standard Mealtimes

Mealtimes in Florence differ greatly from restaurant to restaurant. Most eateries in the city are closed between lunch and dinner, while others only open for business from 1:00pm till late.

Breakfast can be expected from as early as 07:00am to 10:00am. Lunchtime is generally served from 12:00pm to 3:30pm, followed by dinner from 7:00pm to 11:00pm.

Business Hours

Business hours for banks and other public offices in Florence are generally from 8:30am – 1:30pm and 3:00pm – 4:00pm (Mon – Fri). Some offices are open Saturdays from 8:15am – 12:30pm. Business hours for most shops/shopping centres are generally from 3:30pm-8:00pm on Mondays; 10:00am – 8:00pm Tuesday to Friday; 10:00am – 5:30pm on Saturday.

Key Closure Days

Banks and public offices are closed on Sundays and National Holidays. Museums and other Historic buildings alternate closure times to avoid being closed on the same day. You will find that some are closed on Sunday while others are closed on Monday.

Religious holidays are revered as well as Labour Day and Immaculate Conception Day. Holidays that fall on a weekend are observed on that day and no weekdays are given in lieu.

11

Italian Language Essentials

Sunny summer day. Florence, Italy

Italian is spoken by around sixty two million people globally and is the official language of Italy and one of the four national languages of Switzerland. Most travelers find it easy to pick up basic Italian because much of the vocabulary is similar to its English counterpart, such as museo (museum), studente (student), generale (general), parco (park), banca (bank) and so forth. Below, you will find a few common Italian phrases which you can use in everyday situations during your travels!

Greetings

Hello! – Salve! (*sAH-lveh*)

Good morning! – Buon giorno! (*bwon zhor-no*)

Good night – Buona notte! *(bwoh-nah noht-the)*

Hi! – Ciao! *(chow)*

Good Evening! Buona sera! *(bwoh-nah seh-rah)*

How are you? – Come sta? *(koh-meh STA?)*

Do you speak Italian? - Parla italiano? *(par-lah ee-tahl-ee-ah-no)*

What is the matter? - Cosa c'è? *(koh-zah cheh)*

Thank you very much – Grazie millie *(graht-zee-eh mee-leh)*

What is your name? – Come si chiama? *(KOH-meh see kee-AH-mah?)*

Where are you from? – Di dov'e sei? *(dee doh-veh seh-ee)*

OK! – Va bene! *(vah beh-neh)*

Directions

Where? – Dove? *(Doh-VEH)*

Where is the bus? – Dov'e l'autobus? *(doh-VEH low-TOH-boos)*

Where is the train? - Dov'e il treno? *(DOH-veh eel*

TREH-no)

How do I get to _____ Come si arriva a_____ (Koh-meh see ahr-REE-vah ah...?)

Hotel –albergo (ahl-BER-go)

Restaurants – ristoranti *(rees-toh-RAHN-tee)*

Straight ahead – diritto (*dee-REET-toh*)

Street – strada (*STRAH-dah*)

Turn left – Si gira a sinistra (*EE-ree ah see-NEES-trah*)

Turn right – Si gira a destra (*EE-ree ah DEHS-trah*)

Past the – dopo il (*DOH-poh eel*)

Before the –prima del *(PREE-mah dehl)*

North – nord (*nohrd*)

South – sud (*sood*)

East -est (*ehst*)

West ovest (*OH-vehst*)

Please take me to___. Per favore, mi porti a _____ (*pehr fah-VOH-reh, mee POHR-tee ah*)

Stop here, please! – Ferma qui, per favore! (*FEHR-mah kwee pehr fah-VOH-reh*)

I'm in a hurry! – Vado di fretta! (*VAH-doh dee FREHT-tah)*

At the restaurant

I'm a vegetarian – Sono vegetariano/a (*SOH-noh veh-jeh-tah-RYAH-noh/ ah*)

I don't eat beef. – Non mangio il manzo. (*nohn MAHN-joh eel MAHN-dzoh*)

I don't eat pork. – Non mangio il maiale. (*nohn MAHN-joh eel mah-YAH-leh*)

Lunch – il pranzo (*eel PRAHN-dzoh*)

Chicken – il pollo (*eel POHL-loh*)

Fish – il pesce (*eel PEH-sheh*)

Beef – il manzo (*eel MAHN-dzoh*)

Sausage – salsiccia (*sahl-SEET-chah*)

Salad – insalata (*een-sah-LAH-tah*)

Eggs – uova (*WOH-vah*)

Cheese – formaggio (*fohr-MAHD-joh*)

The juice – il succo (*eel SOOK-koh*)

The beer – la birra (*lah beer-RAH*)

Excuse me, waiter? – Scusi, cameriere? (*SKOO-zee, kah-meh-RYEH-reh?*)

Please clear the table. Potete pulire il tavolo, per favore ((*poh-TEH-teh poo-LEE-reh eel tah-VOH-loh, pehr fah-VOH-reh*)

It was delicious. È squisito (*EH skwee-ZEE-toh*)

I'm done. Ho finito (*oh fee-NEE-toh*)

One more, please. Un altro, per favore (*oon AHL-troh, pehr fah-VOH-reh*)

Shopping

Expensive— caro (*KAH-roh*)

I am looking for something cheaper. Cerco qualcosa di più economico (*CHEHR-koh KWAHL-koh-zah dee pyoo eh-koh-NOH-mee-koh*)

OK, I'll take it. Va bene, lo prendo. (*vah BEH-neh, loh PREHN-doh*)

Want to take your Italian a step further?

The internet provides a great opportunity to get to know the Italian language. There are several free sites that can help you navigate your way through some simple phrases and allow you to listen to how Italian is spoken. Try www.oneworlditaliano.com. The BBC also offers a great online Italian course for free with helpful phrases, the Italian alphabet and links to Italian classes and courses. You can find it at http://www.bbc.co.uk/languages/italian/.

12

Florence Top 20 Things to Do

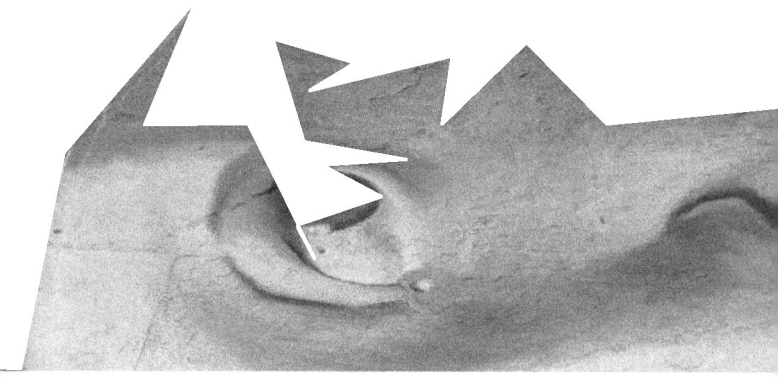

Street Atrist Drawing a Portrait on the Pavement

Finding something interesting to do in Florence may prove to be quite a trick as you will be spoilt for choice by the many things it has to offer. From the beautiful museums and historic art galleries to its overwhelming lunch spots and drinking dens, you're guaranteed a great experience. Here is a list of 20 of our best picks on things to do in Florence.

The **Cathedral of St Mary of the Flower** is the main church of Florence. It dominates the city's Skyline. Open on weekdays 10am – 5pm, currently closed until November 2015.

http://www.museumflorence.com/monuments/1-cathedral

Climbing to the top of the **Dome** to glimpse the amazing views of Florence is open Mon-Fri 8:30 am – 7pm.

http://www.museumflorence.com/monuments/2-dome

The **Baptistery** is one of the most important religious buildings in Florence, dedicated to his patron, St John the Baptist. It is filled with religious historic art. Open Sundays and 1st Saturday of each month, 11:15 am – 7pm. http://www.museumflorence.com/monuments/3-baptistry

Giotto's Bell Tower can be seen from the top of the Duome, it is a beautiful historic monument of costly inventions built by artist after artist who did not live to see its completion. Open Mon to Fri 8:30am to 7pm. http://www.museumflorence.com/monuments/4-bell-tower

In the **Crypt of Santa Reparata** lies Florence's past Bishops in their tombs. A must see. Open weekdays 10am – 5pm, closed on Sundays. http://www.museumflorence.com/monuments/5-crypt

Architectural masterpiece describes best the **Duomo**. Arrive early to have a look at this majestic and historic Centre of the city. Open 10am – 5pm Mon –Wed, Fri; 10am – 4pm, Thurs; 10am – 4:45, Sat; 10am -3:30pm, Sun; Admission Free. http://operaduomo.firenze.it/

The **Uffizi** gallery is by far the greatest treasure trove of eye gorging Renaissance art in the world. Hours on end may be spent here taking in the beauty of art. Open 8:15am – 6:50pm Tues-Sunday.

http://www.uffizi.firenze.it/

Pick up some unique jewelry within **Alessandro Dari's** stunning creations while on the Ponte Vecchio Bridge. Open 9:30 – 1:30pm, 2:30 – 7pm Mon-Fri. http://www.alessandrodari.com/ita-corsi.php

Tickle your taste buds in tasting Florence's most locally preserved wines at the **Vivanda**. This place boasts an extensive list of over 120 wine labels from across Italy to the rest of the world. Open 10:30am - 3pm, 6pm – Midnight Daily. http://www.vivandafirenze.it/home_eng.html

Dine al fresco at **4 Leoni**. Many local eateries have outdoor terraces in Florence but this one stands out. If you are lucky you may get to catch a poetry session on certain nights. Open every day 12am – 12pm. (Piazza della Passera)

http://www.4leoni.com/

Pizza at **O'Munaciello** (via Mafia 31, in the Oltrano area) is quite an experience. Tourists can try out the 7 seasons Pizza which is topped with whatever the Chef of the day finds appealing. Open every day 7pm – 1am.

http://www.munaciello.com/?lang=en

Visit Florence's prettiest church **Santa Maria Novella,** the church is full of painted arches and art worth looking at. Open every day, 9:00 am – 5pm, including public and religious holidays.

http://www.visitflorence.com/florence-churches/santa-maria-novella.html

Break away from the crowds in the city and enjoy the sweeping views in the **Boboli Gardens**. Follow endless paths that you past grand fountains to Palatine Gallery. Open every day 8:15am to 4:30 pm (Nov-Feb); to 5:30 pm (March); to 6:30 pm (April, May, Sept-Oct).

http://www.uffizi.firenze.it/musei/?m=boboli

Not many who visit Florence know about this prenominal chapel, **Pazzi Chapel**. Tourists can look forward to one of the best examples of Renaissance architecture. Open Weekdays 8:15am – 6:50pm, Holidays and Sundays 8:15 – 6:50 pm. Closed on Mondays. http://www.museumsinflorence.com/musei/Pazzi_chapel.html

Palazzo Vecchio is the old town hall of Florence. The intriguing interior features beautifully decorated rooms with wall tapestries and carved doors. Open Fri-Wed 9am- 7pm, Thurs 9am – 2pm. http://www.visitflorence.com/florence-monuments/palazzo-vecchio.html

San Maniato al Monte is situated on a hill just outside Florence. The views of the city from up here are unsurpassed. Open every day 8am -1pm, 3:30 pm – 7pm. http://www.sanminiatoalmonte.it/

Centro Storico is beautiful by day and enchanting by night. Walk along history. Open every day 24h. http://www.firenzealloggio.com/

Another great climb to a fantastic view is on the **Cupola del Brunelleschi**. Open weekdays 8:30 – 7pm. http://www.ilgrandemuseodelduomo.it/monumenti/2-cupola

The **Arno River** is a wonderful way to spend time in Florence and it's common to see the rowing club gliding along the river. Free Admission. http://www.florenceinferno.com/arno-river/

Mercato Centrale is a great spot to pick up gifts for loved ones back home at reasonable prices. Open daily. http://www.mercatocentrale.it/en/mercato-centrale-firenze/

13
Conclusion

Lanes of the old city. Florence, Italy

Most travelers want to make their trip their own with a little sage advice and a few recommendations thrown in for good measure. It has never been easier to research a trip than it is today, so it's a good idea to look closely at hotel reviews, compare flight prices, and plan a few lovely dinners ahead of time. The ubiquitous travel guide is invaluable, helping you to pare down the essentials.

If one thing is for certain, you'll find your own Florence when you arrive. It is a place that strikes everyone differently and it never disappoints. You will eat well, shop often, walk for days, and then bring home the imprints of all the things that dazzled. It's hard to know what you will remember best—the art, food, wine, or its tremendous history. Most people bundle every memory up and create their own everlasting image of Firenze.